Playful Animals
DOLPHINS

Ursula Pang

PowerKiDS press

PK Beginners

Dolphins are playful!

Dolphins live in water.

Dolphins live in groups.

Dolphins talk to each other.

Dolphins eat fish.

Dolphins swim fast.

Dolphins love to jump!

Orcas are the biggest dolphins.

Dolphins do tricks.

Dolphins like to smile.

Dolphins love people!

Published in 2025 by The Rosen Publishing Group, Inc.
2544 Clinton Street, Buffalo, NY 14224

Copyright © 2025 by The Rosen Publishing Group, Inc.

All rights reserved. No part of this book may be reproduced in any form without permission in writing from the publisher, except by a reviewer.

First Edition

Editor: Greg Roza
Book Design: Michael Flynn

Photo Credits: Cover, p. 1 Joe Stone/Shutterstock.com; p. 3 Evgheni Manciu/Shutterstock.com; p. 5 toshiharu_arakawa/Shutterstock.com; p. 7 F Photography R/Shutterstock.com; p. 9 Croisy/Shutterstock.com; p. 11 Svetlana Orusova/Shutterstock.com; p. 13 Four Oaks/Shutterstock.com; p. 15 Photoroyalty/Shutterstock.com; p. 17 slowmotiongli/Shutterstock.com; p. 19 Garmasheva Natalia/Shutterstock.com; p. 21 Andrea Izzotti/Shutterstock.com; p. 23 skvalval/Shutterstock.com.

Library of Congress Cataloging-in-Publication Data

Names: Pang, Ursula, author.
Title: Dolphins / Ursula Pang.
Description: [New York] : PowerKids Press, [2025] | Series: Playful animals
Identifiers: LCCN 2024028037 (print) | LCCN 2024028038 (ebook) | ISBN 9781499450743 (library binding) | ISBN 9781499450736 (paperback) | ISBN 9781499450750 (ebook)
Subjects: LCSH: Dolphins–Juvenile literature.
Classification: LCC QL737.C432 P355 2025 (print) | LCC QL737.C432 (ebook) | DDC 599.53–dc23/eng/20240627
LC record available at https://lccn.loc.gov/2024028037
LC ebook record available at https://lccn.loc.gov/2024028038

Manufactured in the United States of America

Some of the images in this book illustrate individuals who are models. The depictions do not imply actual situations or events.

CPSIA Compliance Information: Batch #CWPK25. For further information contact Rosen Publishing at 1-800-237-9932.